# Making a Garden

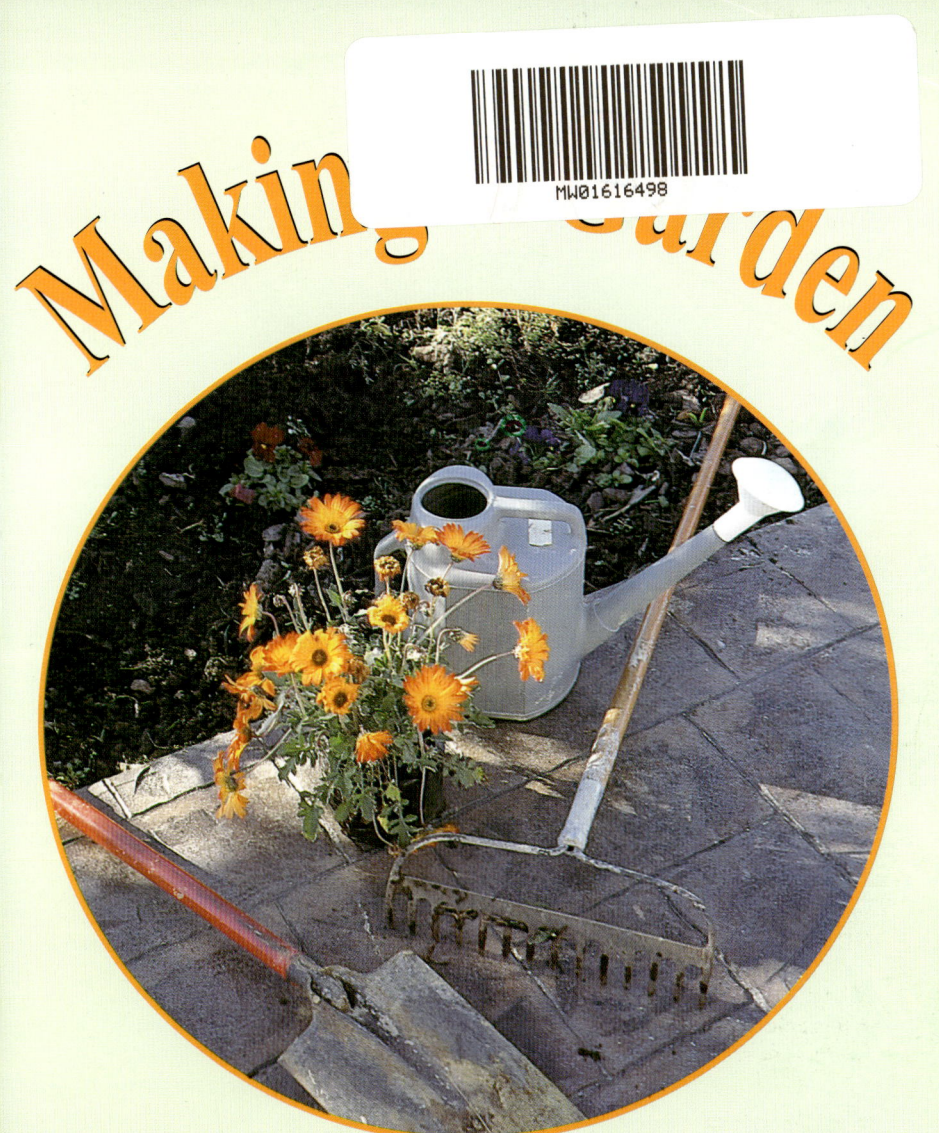

**Written by Tracey Reeder**

**Photographed by Dean Iversen**

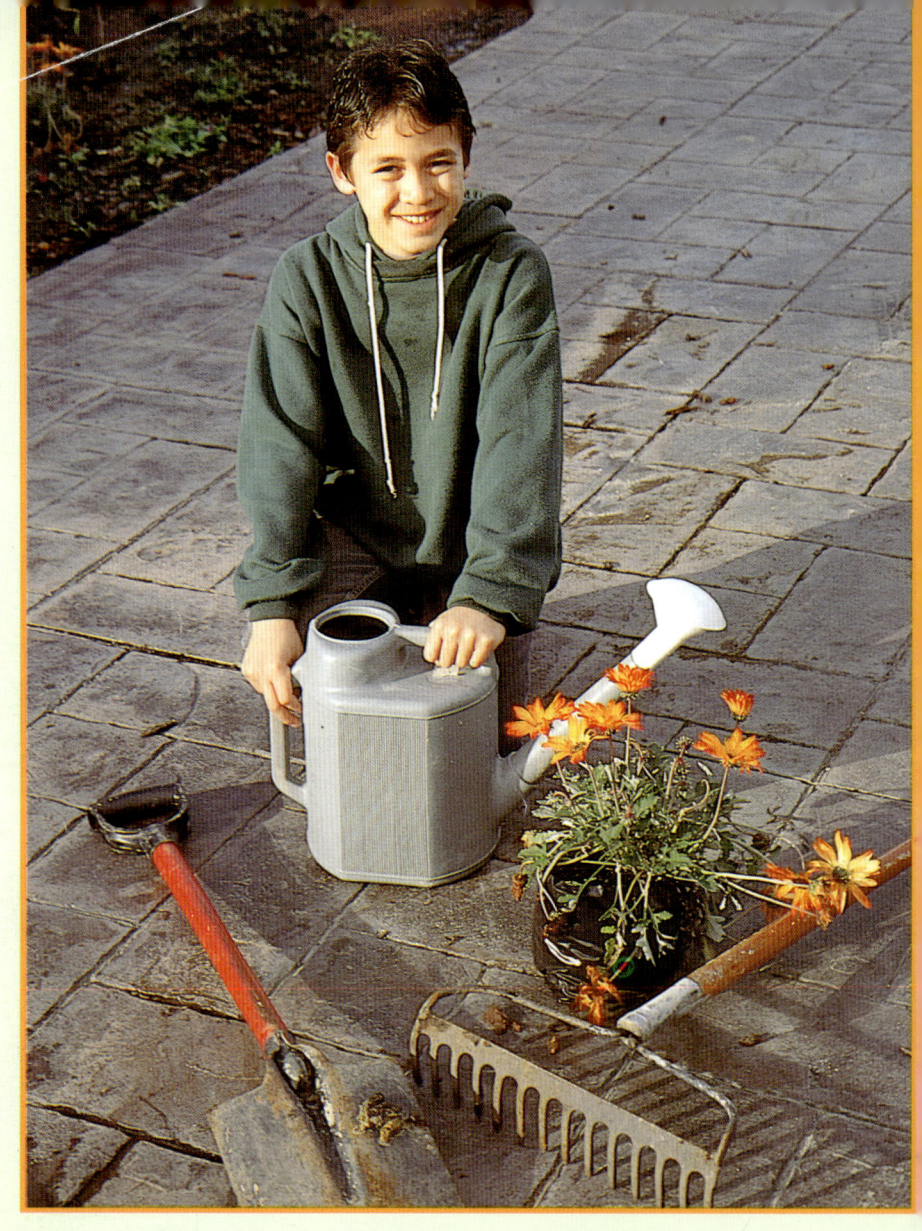

# Here is the gardener.

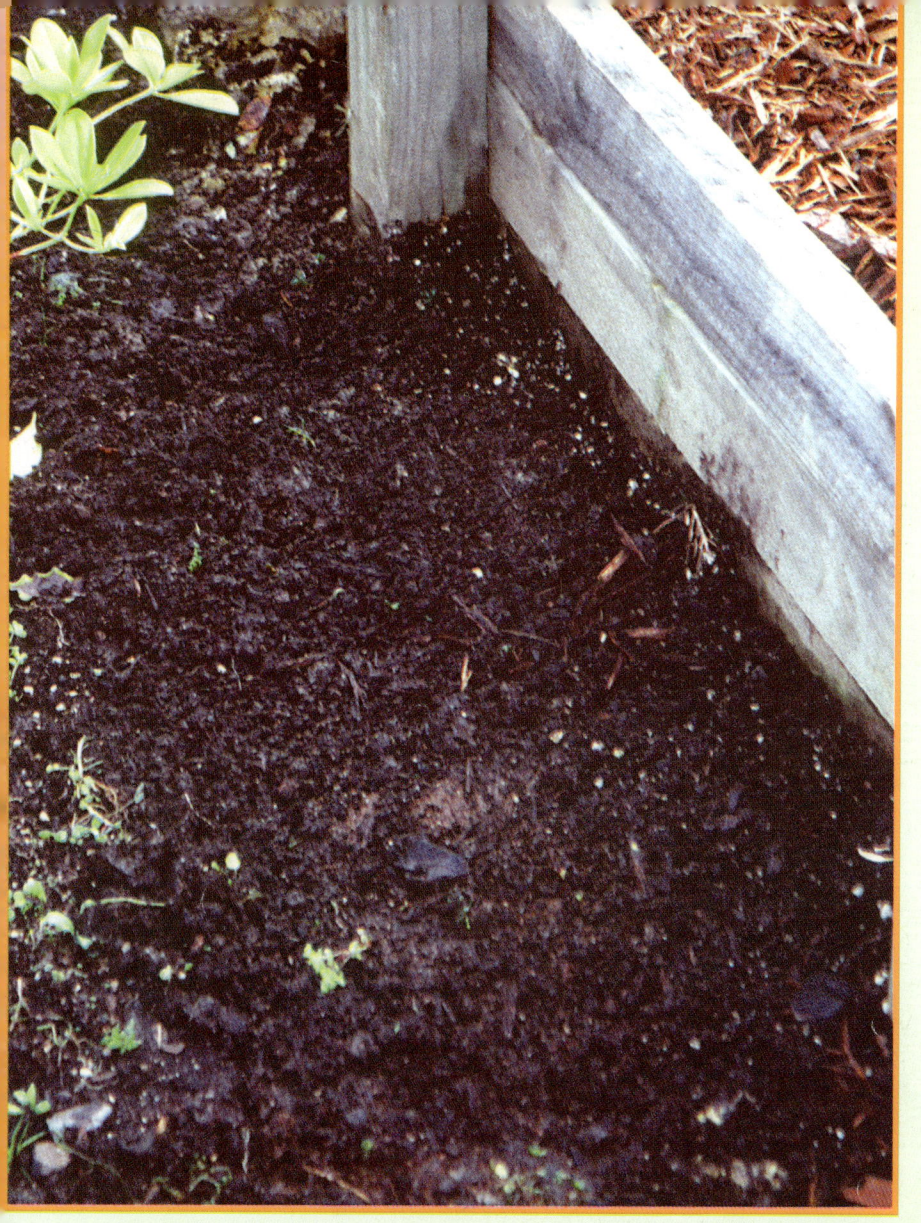

Here is the dirt.

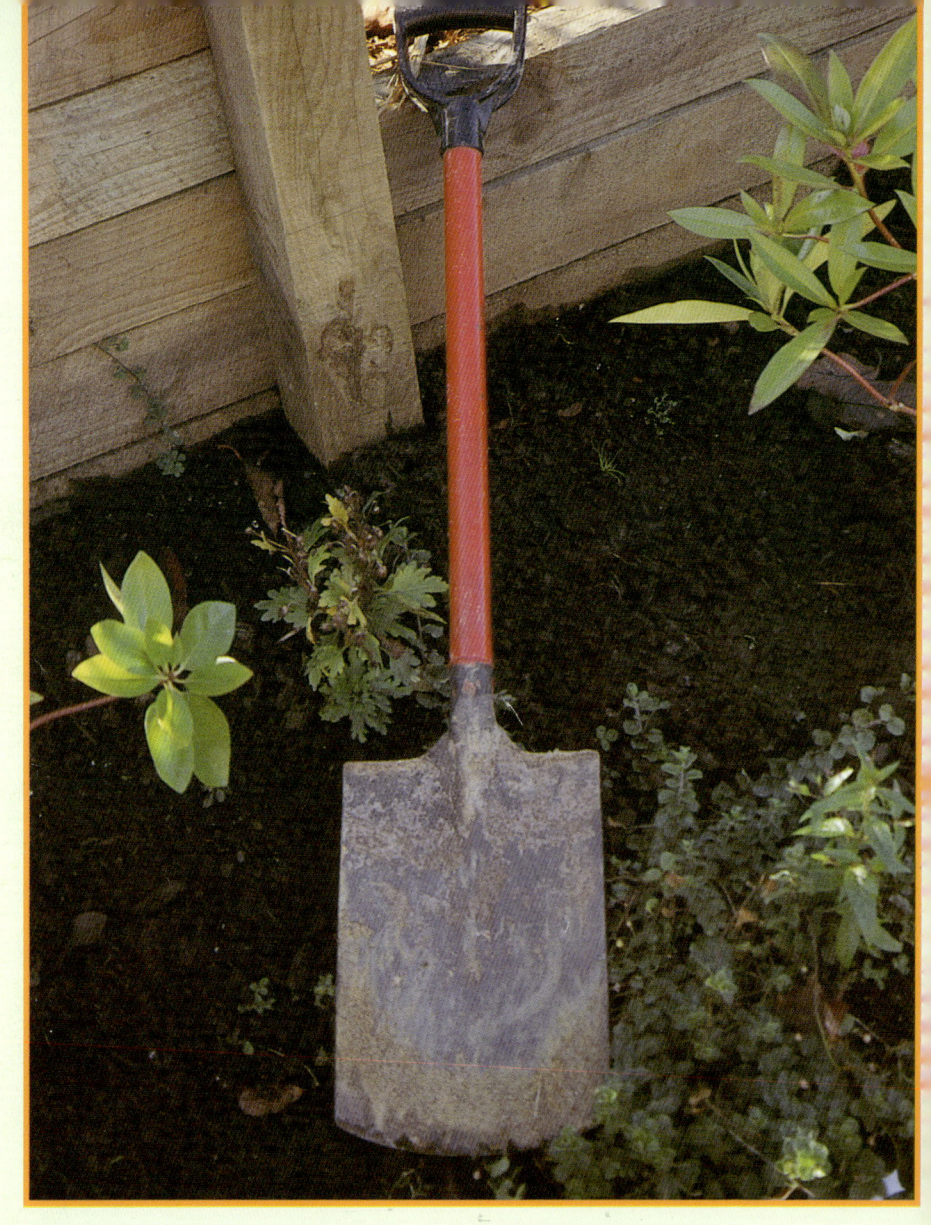

Here is the shovel.

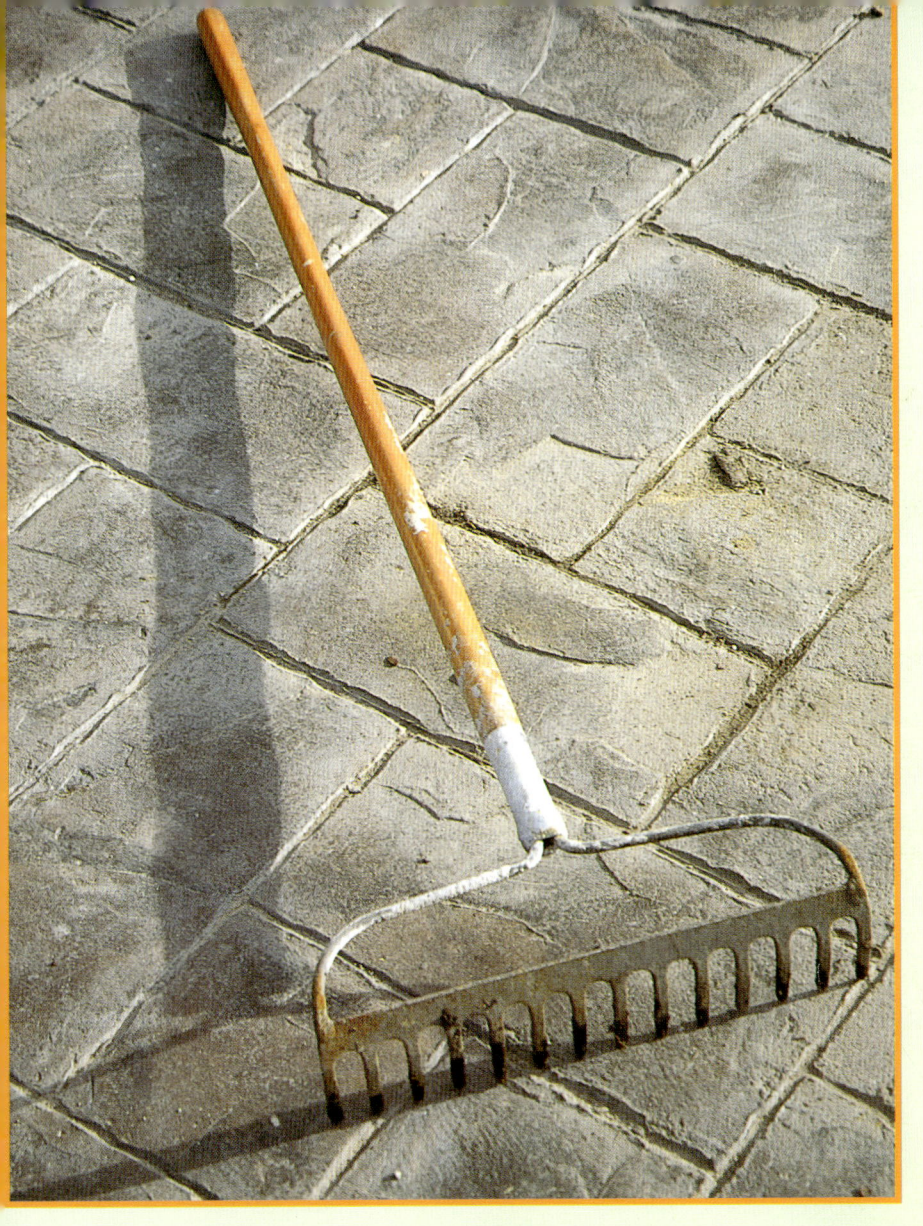

Here is the rake.

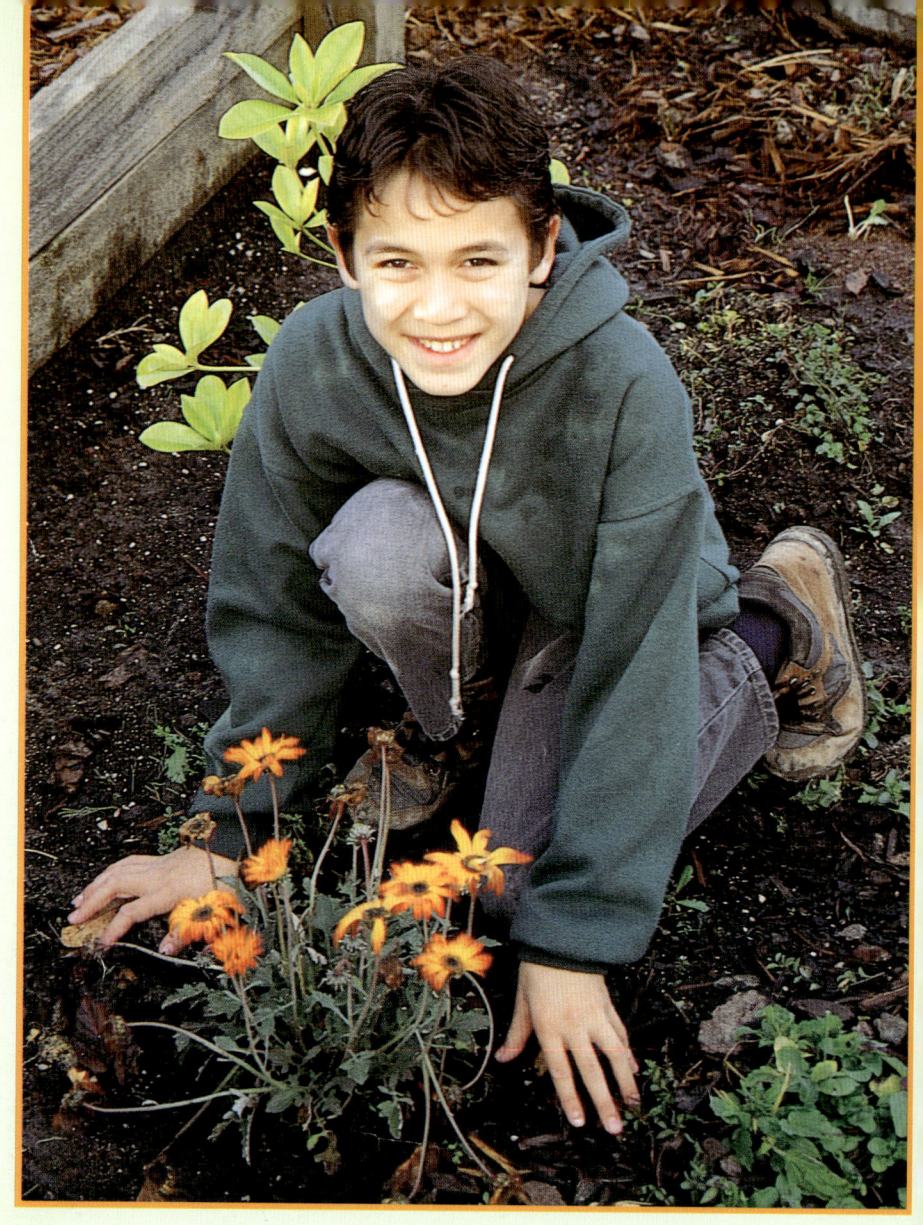

Here is the plant.

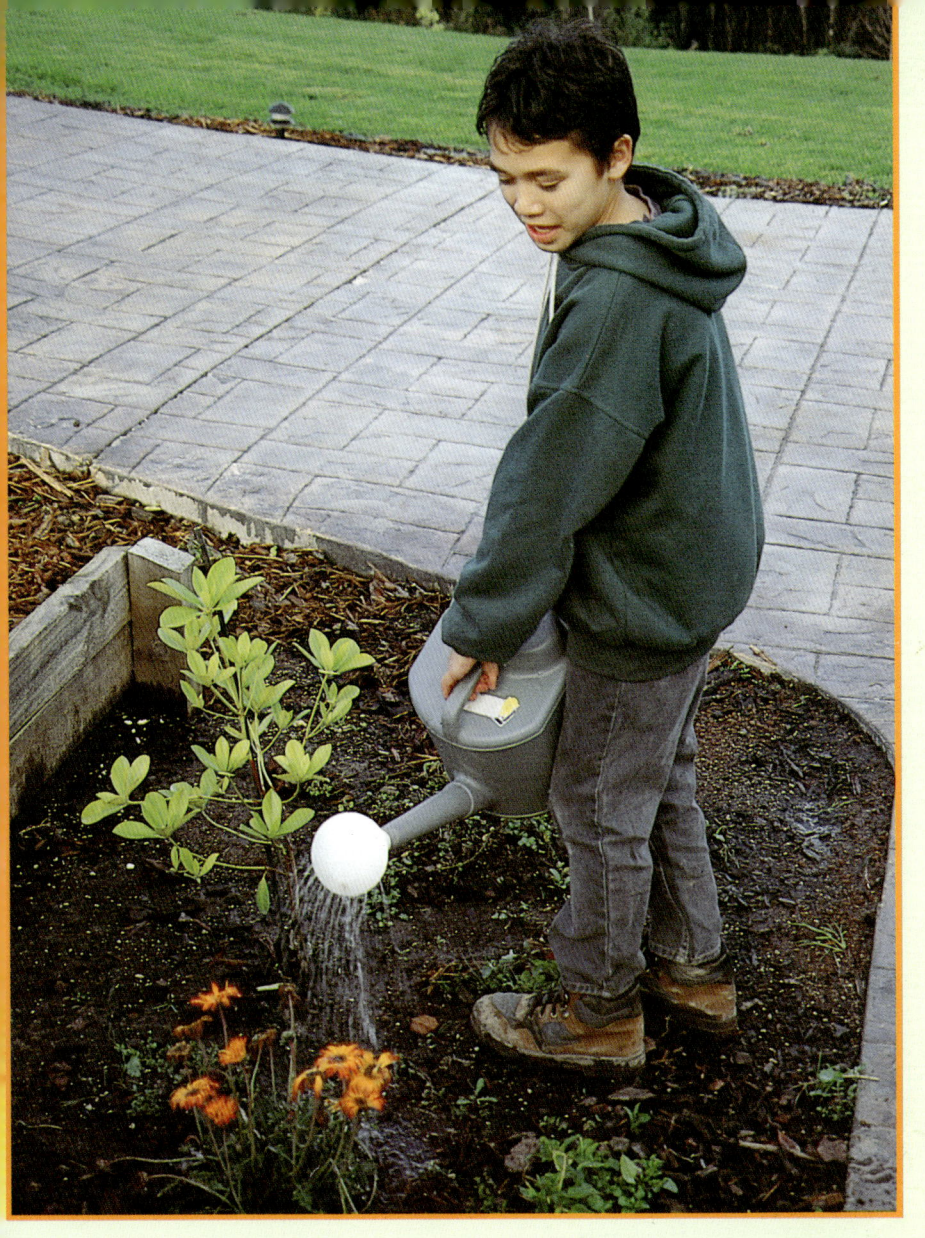

Here is the water.

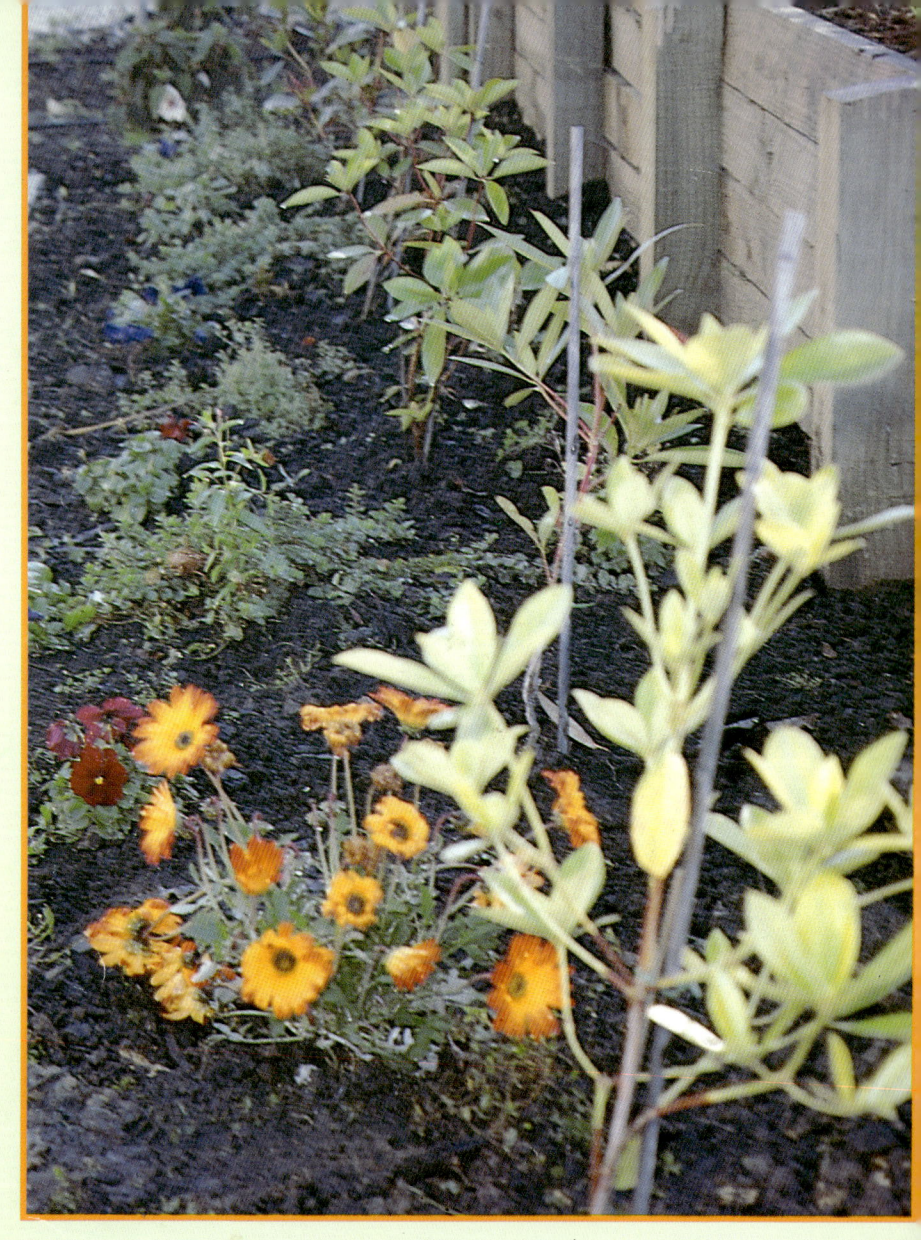

Here is the garden.